Medical Tyranny: How Covid-19 Has Been Used to Suppress Our Freedoms

Michael Morton

Published by Michael Morton, 2023.

Also by Michael Morton

Personal Autonomy Now!
Situational Awareness

Standalone
How To Raise An Alpha Child
52 Weeks to a New You! A One-Year Plan To Improve and Change Your Life
Medical Tyranny: How Covid-19 Has Been Used to Suppress Our Freedoms
Guía de Supervivencia Urbana
Guide de Survie en Milieu Urbain en Période de Turbulences
El Auge de la Ola Roja: La expansión de los Gobiernos Socialistas en Sudamérica

Table of Contents

Introduction

The COVID-19 pandemic has brought about unprecedented changes in our daily lives, from the way we work and socialize to the way we travel and access healthcare. While some of these changes were necessary to contain the spread of the virus, others have been used to suppress our freedoms and rights. This book explores how the pandemic has been used as an excuse to implement medical tyranny, a system of control that undermines our civil liberties, constitutional rights, and the principles of democracy.

Medical tyranny is not a new concept. Throughout history, governments and authorities have used medical emergencies to justify the suspension of individual freedoms and the imposition of authoritarian measures. However, the COVID-19 pandemic has provided the perfect storm for the rise of medical tyranny on a global scale. The fear and panic generated by the virus, the misinformation spread by mainstream media, and the inconsistencies and contradictions in COVID-19 policies and guidelines have created an environment where tyranny can thrive.

In this book, we will examine the various facets of medical tyranny and how they have impacted our lives. We will explore the role of fear and panic in controlling the masses, the politicization of science, the dangers of emergency powers and executive orders, the erosion of civil liberties and constitutional rights, and the use of technology and surveillance to monitor and control the population. We will also look at the resistance movement, the voices of doctors, scientists, and citizens who are standing up against medical tyranny.

Finally, we will discuss the future of medical tyranny and what we can do about it. We will explore the importance of transparency, accountability, and freedom in medical practices and policies. We will also discuss the need for a paradigm shift in public health approaches and the importance of empowering individuals to make informed decisions about their health.

Chapter 1

The Rise of Medical Tyranny

The term "medical tyranny" refers to a system of control in which medical authorities and government officials use health emergencies to justify the imposition of authoritarian measures. While medical emergencies can indeed require exceptional measures to contain and manage them, medical tyranny occurs when such measures go beyond what is necessary and reasonable. The roots of medical tyranny can be traced back to the early days of public health.

In the 19th century, governments around the world began to establish public health measures to prevent the spread of infectious diseases. These measures included quarantine, isolation, and vaccination. While many of these measures were effective in controlling the spread of diseases, they also raised concerns about individual liberties and rights. In the 20th century, medical tyranny took on a new dimension

In the 20th century, medical tyranny took on a new dimension with the rise of totalitarian regimes such as Nazi Germany and Soviet Russia. These regimes used medical science as a tool of control, using it to justify eugenics, forced sterilization, and other atrocities. The legacy of these regimes is a warning of the dangers of medical tyranny and the need to be vigilant against its reemergence. In recent years, medical tyranny has been on the rise in many parts of the world.

Governments and medical authorities have been using public health emergencies to impose authoritarian measures such as lockdowns, mandatory vaccinations, and travel restrictions. These measures have been justified on the grounds of protecting public health, but they have also raised concerns about individual freedoms and rights. The COVID-19 pandemic has been a catalyst for the rise of medical tyranny on a global scale.

The pandemic has been used as a pretext for the imposition of emergency measures that have undermined civil liberties and constitutional rights. These measures include lockdowns, mandatory mask-wearing, and social distancing rules. While some of these measures may have been necessary in the early stages of the pandemic, their continuation has raised questions about their effectiveness and proportionality. The response to the pandemic has also highlighted the politicization of science and the use of science as a tool of control. Scientific experts have been used to justify policy decisions that are often inconsistent and contradictory.

The media has played a significant role in spreading fear and misinformation, leading to public confusion and anxiety. The rise of medical tyranny has significant implications for democracy and individual freedoms. In a democratic society, citizens have the right to participate in policy decisions that affect their lives. Medical tyranny undermines this principle by using medical emergencies as a pretext for the imposition of authoritarian measures without democratic oversight or accountability.

In the coming chapters, we will examine the various aspects of medical tyranny and how they have impacted our lives. We will look at the role of fear and panic in controlling the masses, the impact of lockdowns on mental health and societal well-being, the politicization of science, and the dangers of executive powers and emergency orders. We will also examine the erosion of civil liberties and constitutional rights and the use of technology and surveillance to monitor and control the population.

Overall, this chapter has highlighted the historical context and current reality of medical tyranny, as well as its implications for individual freedoms and democracy. The following chapters will delve deeper into each aspect of medical tyranny and explore the ways in which it has been used during the COVID-19 pandemic.

Chapter 2

The COVID-19 Pandemic: The Perfect Storm for Tyranny

The COVID-19 pandemic has been a global health crisis unlike anything the world has seen in modern times. The virus has infected millions of people, resulting in hundreds of thousands of deaths. The pandemic has also had a significant impact on economies, societies, and individual lives. While the pandemic has been a real and serious threat, it has also been used as a pretext for the imposition of authoritarian measures.

Governments and medical authorities have used the pandemic to justify lockdowns, travel restrictions, mandatory mask-wearing, and other measures that have undermined civil liberties and constitutional rights. One reason why the pandemic has been so conducive to the rise of medical tyranny is the fear and panic that it has generated. Fear and panic are powerful emotions that can be used to manipulate people and control their behavior. In the case of COVID-19, fear and panic have been used to justify extreme measures that may not be necessary or effective. Another reason why the pandemic has been so conducive to medical tyranny is the speed with which it has spread.

The pandemic has spread rapidly around the world, leading to a sense of urgency and the need for immediate action. This urgency has been used to justify emergency measures that bypass normal democratic processes and oversight. The pandemic has also highlighted the global interconnectedness of the world and the need for coordinated responses to global crises. However, the response to the pandemic has also highlighted the tensions between national sovereignty and global cooperation.

The COVID-19 pandemic has been the perfect storm for the rise of medical tyranny. The fear and panic generated by the virus, the urgency of the situation, and the tensions between national sovereignty and global cooperation have all contributed to the imposition of authoritarian measures. In the following chapters, we will examine the various aspects of medical tyranny during the pandemic and their implications for democracy and individual freedoms.

Chapter 3

How Fear and Panic Were Used to Control the Masses

The COVID-19 pandemic has been a time of fear and uncertainty for many people. The rapid spread of the virus and the high mortality rate in some countries contributed to a sense of impending doom. In response, governments and medical authorities around the world implemented extreme measures to control the spread of the virus. One of the most significant factors in the implementation of these measures has been fear and panic. Fear and panic are powerful emotions that can be used to manipulate people and control their behavior.

During the pandemic, fear and panic were used to justify extreme measures such as lockdowns, mandatory mask-wearing, and social distancing rules. The media played a significant role in spreading fear and panic during the pandemic. Sensationalist headlines, alarmist reporting, and the constant repetition of COVID-19 statistics contributed to a sense of anxiety and uncertainty. The media also played a role in disseminating misinformation, leading to public confusion and mistrust. Governments and medical authorities also contributed to the spread of fear and panic. Official statements and press conferences often emphasized worst-case scenarios, leading to a sense of impending doom. The use of alarming language, such as "war" and "battle," also contributed to a sense of crisis and urgency.

While fear and panic may have been necessary to some extent to raise public awareness and encourage compliance with public health measures, they also had negative consequences. Fear and panic can lead to irrational behavior and decision-making, such as hoarding and panic buying. They can also lead to social and psychological harm, such as anxiety, depression, and trauma. Furthermore, the use of fear and panic as a tool of control is not a new phenomenon.

Throughout history, governments and authorities have used fear and panic to justify authoritarian measures. The COVID-19 pandemic is no exception, and the use of fear and panic has been a significant factor in the rise of medical tyranny. In the coming chapters, we will examine the ways in which fear and panic were used to justify extreme measures during the pandemic. We will also examine the implications of this approach for democracy and individual freedoms. The use of fear and panic as a tool of control raises significant ethical and moral questions that must be addressed in the context of public health emergencies.

Chapter 4

The Role of Mainstream Media in Spreading Fear and Misinformation

The COVID-19 pandemic has been a time of unprecedented uncertainty and fear for many people. The rapid spread of the virus, the high mortality rate, and the lack of effective treatments and vaccines have contributed to a sense of anxiety and hopelessness. In response, governments and medical authorities around the world implemented extreme measures to control the spread of the virus.

One of the key factors in the implementation of these measures has been fear and panic, which have been fueled, in part, by mainstream media reporting. Sensationalist headlines, alarmist reporting, and the constant repetition of COVID-19 statistics have contributed to a sense of anxiety and uncertainty. Furthermore, the media has often disseminated misinformation, leading to public confusion and mistrust. Sensationalist reporting is a common tactic used by mainstream media to attract viewers or readers.

Sensationalist reporting focuses on the most extreme and dramatic aspects of a story, often ignoring nuance and complexity. During the pandemic, sensationalist reporting has contributed to a sense of crisis and urgency, leading to the perception that extreme measures are necessary to control the virus. This has led to a sense of fear and panic among the public, which has been used to justify authoritarian measures. Another way in which the media has contributed to the spread of fear and panic is through the constant repetition of COVID-19 statistics. While it is important to report on the number of cases and deaths, the constant repetition of these statistics can create a sense of doom and hopelessness.

The media has also been criticized for focusing on negative news stories while ignoring positive developments, leading to a skewed perception of the pandemic. Misinformation has also been a significant problem during the pandemic. The media has been a significant source of misinformation, often reporting on unverified claims and speculation. This has led to public confusion and mistrust, as people struggle to distinguish between fact and fiction.

Misinformation can be dangerous during a public health emergency, as it can lead to ineffective or harmful responses. Moreover, the media has often failed to provide context and perspective on the pandemic. By focusing on individual cases and stories, the media has created a distorted view of the pandemic that ignores broader trends and patterns. This has contributed to a sense of anxiety and uncertainty, as people struggle to understand the true nature of the pandemic.

The role of the mainstream media in shaping public perceptions and attitudes during the COVID-19 pandemic has been a mixed one. While the media has played an important role in raising public awareness of the virus, it has also contributed to the spread of fear and misinformation. In the coming chapters, we will examine the ways in which the media has influenced public perceptions and attitudes during the pandemic, and the implications of this influence for democracy and individual freedoms.

Chapter 5

The Inconsistencies and Contradictions in COVID-19 Policies and Guidelines

The COVID-19 pandemic has undoubtedly disrupted our lives in many ways. As the virus continues to spread, governments and organizations around the world have implemented various policies and guidelines to combat its spread. However, as time has gone on, it has become increasingly clear that these policies and guidelines are often inconsistent and contradictory, leading to confusion and frustration among the general public.

One of the most glaring examples of inconsistency in COVID-19 policies is the issue of mask-wearing. At the beginning of the pandemic, many public health officials stated that masks were not necessary for the general public and should be reserved for healthcare workers. However, as more information became available, guidelines changed, and many officials began recommending the use of masks in public spaces.

Despite this change in guidance, many governments have been slow to adopt mask mandates, and some have even gone as far as to actively discourage mask-wearing. For example, in the United States, some governors have refused to issue mask mandates, citing concerns over personal freedoms and the economy. This lack of consistency has led to confusion among the public and has likely contributed to the continued spread of the virus.

Another area of inconsistency in COVID-19 policies is the issue of school closures. At the beginning of the pandemic, many schools around the world were closed in an effort to slow the spread of the virus. However, as time has gone on, there has been increasing pressure to reopen schools, as many parents and educators worry about the long-term effects of prolonged school closures on students.

Despite this pressure, many governments have been slow to reopen schools, citing concerns over the potential spread of the virus in a classroom setting. This has led to frustration among parents and educators, who feel that the guidelines for school closures are inconsistent and unclear.

Perhaps one of the most significant examples of inconsistency in COVID-19 policies is the issue of travel restrictions. Many governments around the world have implemented strict travel restrictions, limiting the movement of people in and out of certain countries in an effort to slow the spread of the virus. However, these restrictions are often arbitrary and unclear, leading to confusion and frustration among travelers.

For example, some countries have banned travelers from certain countries entirely, while others have implemented mandatory quarantine periods for travelers from certain regions. In some cases, these restrictions have been lifted or changed without warning, leading to confusion and uncertainty among travelers.

These inconsistencies and contradictions in COVID-19 policies and guidelines have led to significant frustration and confusion among the general public. While it is understandable that policies and guidelines may change as more information becomes available, it is essential that governments and organizations work to communicate these changes clearly and consistently to the public.

In addition, it is crucial that policies and guidelines be based on sound scientific evidence and data, rather than political or economic concerns. By doing so, we can ensure that our efforts to combat the spread of COVID-19 are effective, efficient, and consistent.

The COVID-19 pandemic has highlighted the need for clear, consistent, and evidence-based policies and guidelines. As we continue to navigate this unprecedented situation, it is essential that governments and organizations work together to ensure that their policies and guidelines are clear, consistent, and based on the best available scientific evidence. By doing so, we can minimize confusion and frustration among the public, and work together to combat the fear of this virus.

Chapter 6

The Politicalization of Science: How Science Has Been Weaponized to Serve Political Agendas

Science is a critical tool for understanding the world around us and informing policy decisions. However, science can also be easily politicized, especially in areas where there are significant economic or political interests at stake. This can lead to inconsistencies and contradictions in policies and guidelines and can ultimately undermine public trust in science.

One example of this is the politicization of science in the context of the COVID-19 pandemic. Throughout the pandemic, there have been numerous examples of politicians and other public figures using science to advance their own agendas, rather than using it to inform evidence-based policy decisions. This has resulted in a confusing array of policies and guidelines, many of which seem to contradict each other.

This inconsistency in messaging has eroded public trust in the science behind COVID-19 policies and guidelines. It has also created confusion and skepticism about the effectiveness of different interventions, which has made it more difficult to control the spread of the virus.

Another example of the politicization of science is the use of scientific research to advance political agendas. This can manifest in a variety of ways, from selective funding of research that supports a particular political agenda, to censorship of research findings that do not align with political interests.

The politicalization of science has significant consequences for both the scientific community and the public. It undermines the credibility of science as a tool for understanding the world and informing policy decisions, and it can ultimately lead to policies that do not effectively address the issues they are intended to solve.

To address this issue, it is critical to prioritize scientific integrity and ensure that science is not used as a political tool. This means protecting the independence of scientific research, promoting transparency and open access to scientific findings, and supporting evidence-based policy decisions that are guided by scientific research rather than political interests.

Chapter 7

The Dangers of Emergency Powers and Executive Orders

The COVID-19 pandemic has led to the widespread use of emergency powers and executive orders by governments around the world. These powers, which are intended to allow governments to respond quickly and effectively to emergencies, have been used to implement a range of policies and measures aimed at controlling the spread of the virus. However, there are growing concerns about the potential dangers of emergency powers and executive orders, particularly in the context of medical tyranny.

Medical tyranny refers to the use of medical or health-related policies and measures to control and restrict the freedoms of individuals and populations. This can include mandatory vaccination, forced quarantine, and restrictions on movement and assembly. While these measures may be necessary in certain circumstances, they can also be used to suppress dissent and undermine civil liberties.

The use of emergency powers and executive orders can exacerbate these concerns, as they give governments broad authority to implement policies and measures without the normal checks and balances of the legislative process. This can lead to policies that are not fully thought out or that infringe on individual rights and freedoms without due process.

For example, during the COVID-19 pandemic, many governments have implemented mandatory vaccination policies or have used emergency powers to enforce quarantine measures. While these measures may be necessary to control the spread of the virus, they can also be used to suppress dissent and to limit individual freedom.

Moreover, the use of emergency powers and executive orders can also have long-term consequences for democratic institutions and civil liberties. Once emergency powers are invoked, it can be difficult to return to normal democratic processes, and there is a risk that these powers will be abused or extended beyond their intended purpose.

To address these concerns, it is critical to ensure that emergency powers and executive orders are used judiciously and with appropriate checks and balances. This includes ensuring that policies and measures are *evidence-based*, transparent, and subject to review and oversight. It also means promoting open and transparent communication with the public about the rationale for emergency measures and their potential consequences. It is critical to ensure that emergency powers are not used to infringe on individual rights and freedoms without due process. This means ensuring that any restrictions on individual liberties are proportional, necessary, and grounded in evidence-based research.

It is important to recognize that the dangers of medical tyranny and emergency powers are not limited to the COVID-19 pandemic. These issues will continue to be relevant in the context of future emergencies and crises, and it is critical that we work to address them proactively and with the utmost care and attention to protecting individual rights and liberties.

Chapter 8

The Erosion of Civil Liberties and Constitutional Rights

The erosion of civil liberties and constitutional rights is a growing concern in many parts of the world, particularly in the context of emergency situations like pandemics. During times of crisis, governments often take steps to restrict certain rights and freedoms in order to address the emergency situation. However, these measures can sometimes go too far and result in significant restrictions on civil liberties and constitutional rights.

One specific example of the erosion of civil liberties and constitutional rights is the use of surveillance technologies to monitor individuals during the pandemic. In some countries, governments have used drones, facial recognition technology, and mobile phone tracking to monitor individuals and enforce quarantine measures. While these measures may be necessary to control the spread of the virus, they can also be highly invasive and have significant implications for individual privacy and civil liberties.

Another example is the use of emergency powers and executive orders to restrict or suspend certain civil liberties and constitutional rights. In some countries, emergency powers have been used to impose curfews, limit freedom of movement, and restrict access to healthcare and other essential services. While these measures may be necessary to control the spread of the virus, they can also be highly restrictive and have significant implications for individual freedoms and human rights.

A third example is the use of mandatory vaccination policies, which have been proposed or implemented in some countries as a way to control the spread of the virus. While vaccines can be an effective tool for controlling the spread of infectious diseases, mandatory vaccination policies can infringe on individual rights and freedoms, particularly in the absence of informed consent and the availability of alternative treatments.

Overall, the erosion of civil liberties and constitutional rights is a significant concern in the current political climate, particularly in the context of emergency situations like pandemics. It is critical that policymakers and government officials approach these issues with the utmost care and attention to protecting individual rights and freedoms, promoting evidence-based policies and measures, and ensuring that emergency powers are used judiciously and with appropriate checks and balances.

Chapter 9

The Use of Technology and Surveillance to Control and Monitor the Population

The use of technology and surveillance to control and monitor the population has become increasingly common in many parts of the world. While technology and surveillance can be useful tools for addressing public safety and security concerns, they also raise important questions about privacy, civil liberties, and human rights.

One example of the use of technology and surveillance to control and monitor the population is the use of facial recognition technology by law enforcement agencies. In some countries, law enforcement agencies use facial recognition technology to identify and track individuals in real-time, without their consent. While this technology can be useful for identifying suspects in criminal investigations, it can also be highly invasive and have significant implications for individual privacy and civil liberties.

Another example is the use of surveillance technologies to monitor and control public behavior. In some countries, governments use surveillance technologies to monitor public spaces and identify individuals who are engaging in behavior deemed inappropriate or threatening. While this can be useful for ensuring public safety, it can also be highly intrusive and have significant implications for individual freedoms and human rights.

A third example is the use of tracking technologies to monitor individuals during the COVID-19 pandemic. In some countries, governments have used mobile phone tracking, GPS technologies, and other tracking technologies to monitor individuals who have been infected with the virus, as well as those who have been in close contact with infected individuals. While this can be useful for controlling the spread of the virus, it can also be highly intrusive and have significant implications for individual privacy and civil liberties.

Overall, the use of technology and surveillance to control and monitor the population is a complex and multifaceted issue. It is important for policymakers and government officials to approach these issues with care and attention to the protection of individual rights and freedoms, while also taking into account the need for public safety and security. This requires a careful balancing of competing interests and the implementation of appropriate safeguards and regulations to ensure that technology and surveillance are used in a responsible and ethical manner.

The use of technology and surveillance to control and monitor the population has been a topic of increasing concern in recent years. With the advancement of technology, it has become easier for governments and law enforcement agencies to monitor and control the behavior of individuals in real-time, raising important questions about individual privacy and civil liberties.

One of the key concerns with the use of technology and surveillance is the potential for abuse by those in power. In some cases, governments and law enforcement agencies have been known to use surveillance technologies to target individuals based on their political beliefs, religious affiliations, or other personal characteristics. This can result in the violation of individual rights and freedoms and can create a climate of fear and distrust within society.

Another concern is the potential for technology and surveillance to be used to suppress dissent and limit freedom of expression. In some countries, governments have used surveillance technologies to monitor and control the activities of political dissidents, journalists, and activists, leading to widespread censorship and the suppression of free speech.

A third concern is the impact of surveillance on individual privacy. With the proliferation of surveillance cameras, facial recognition technology, and other monitoring tools, individuals are increasingly being monitored and tracked without their knowledge or consent. This can have significant implications for personal privacy and can erode trust between individuals and government institutions.

Despite these concerns, there are also arguments in favor of the use of technology and surveillance for public safety and security purposes. For example, surveillance technologies can be useful for preventing and responding to crime and terrorism and can help to ensure public safety in high-risk areas. Similarly, tracking technologies can be useful for controlling the spread of infectious diseases, as demonstrated during the COVID-19 pandemic.

Ultimately, the use of technology and surveillance to control and monitor the population is a complex issue that requires careful consideration and attention to individual rights and freedoms. Policymakers and government officials must work to strike a balance between the need for public safety and security, and the protection of individual privacy and civil liberties. This requires the implementation of appropriate safeguards and regulations, as well as ongoing monitoring and evaluation to ensure that these technologies are used in a responsible and ethical manner.

Chapter 10

The Push for Mandatory Vaccinations and Vaccine Passports

The push for mandatory vaccinations and vaccine passports has become a controversial issue in many countries, with advocates arguing that they are necessary to protect public health, while opponents argue that they infringe on individual liberties and rights. Here are three examples that illustrate the complexities of this issue:

1. Mandatory Vaccinations for School Children: Many countries require school children to receive certain vaccinations before they can attend school, in order to prevent the spread of diseases such as measles, mumps, and rubella. While some parents may object to these mandatory vaccinations on religious or philosophical grounds, public health officials argue that they are necessary to protect the wider community from outbreaks of disease. However, the COVID-19 pandemic has raised new questions about the efficacy and safety of vaccines, with some individuals expressing concerns about the speed of vaccine development and the potential long-term side effects.

2. Vaccine Passports for Travel and Public Events: In some countries, vaccine passports are being proposed as a way to allow individuals to travel or attend public events, such as concerts or sports games. These passports would provide proof that an individual has been vaccinated against COVID-19, and could be required for entry into certain venues or

countries. While proponents argue that vaccine passports would help to prevent the spread of COVID-19 and allow for a safer return to normal activities, opponents argue that they would create a two-tiered society, with those who have been vaccinated enjoying greater freedoms and privileges than those who have not.

3. Vaccine Mandates for Healthcare Workers: In some countries, healthcare workers are required to receive certain vaccinations as a condition of employment, in order to prevent the spread of diseases within healthcare settings. However, some healthcare workers may object to these mandates on religious or philosophical grounds, or may express concerns about the safety or efficacy of certain vaccines. While public health officials argue that these mandates are necessary to protect vulnerable patients from infectious diseases, opponents argue that they infringe on individual rights and freedoms.

This is a complex issue that raises important questions about individual rights and freedoms, public health, and the role of government in regulating healthcare. While there are arguments in favor of mandatory vaccinations and vaccine passports for certain populations, policymakers and government officials must also consider the potential risks and unintended consequences of these measures, and work to ensure that they are implemented in a fair, ethical, and transparent manner.

The push for mandatory vaccinations and vaccine passports has also raised concerns about potential violations of individual rights and liberties, including those enshrined in the Constitution. Specifically, opponents argue that mandatory vaccinations and vaccine passports could violate the First and Fourth Amendments of the Constitution, which protect freedom of speech, religion, and assembly, as well as privacy rights.

In addition, there have been reports of military members being discharged for refusing to receive the COVID-19 vaccine, which has also raised questions about individual rights and freedoms. While military members are subject to certain vaccination requirements as a condition of service, some argue that mandating the COVID-19 vaccine goes beyond what is necessary to protect national security and represents a violation of individual rights.

Furthermore, opponents of mandatory vaccinations and vaccine passports argue that these measures could have a disproportionate impact on marginalized communities, including those with limited access to healthcare or vaccine education. There are concerns that vaccine mandates could exacerbate existing health disparities and perpetuate systemic inequalities.

On the other hand, proponents of mandatory vaccinations and vaccine passports argue that these measures are necessary to protect public health and prevent the spread of infectious diseases, particularly in the context of a global pandemic. They argue that individual rights and freedoms must be balanced against the collective good, and that vaccine mandates are a necessary and reasonable public health measure.

The debate over mandatory vaccinations and vaccine passports is complex and raises important questions about individual rights and liberties, as well as public health and safety. While mandatory vaccinations and vaccine passports may be necessary in some circumstances, policymakers and government officials must also ensure that these measures are implemented in a way that is consistent with the Constitution and protects individual rights and freedoms. Additionally, military members who refuse the vaccine should not be discharged for refusing a vaccine which was not widely tested before its implementation.

Chapter 11

The Resistance:
Voices of Doctors, Scientists, and Citizens Against Medical Tyranny

The resistance against medical tyranny has been growing in recent times, with doctors, scientists, and citizens alike speaking out against the encroachment on individual rights and liberties in the name of public health.

One notable voice in the resistance is Dr. Robert Malone, a physician and inventor of the mRNA vaccine technology, who has been critical of the rush to vaccinate the entire population without proper testing and evaluation. He has expressed concern about potential long-term side effects of the COVID-19 vaccines and has called for more transparency and data sharing in the decision-making process.

Similarly, Dr. Peter McCullough, a renowned cardiologist and internist, has been outspoken in his criticism of the vaccine rollout and the suppression of alternative treatments for COVID-19, such as hydroxychloroquine and ivermectin. He has also raised concerns about the censorship of medical information and the silencing of dissenting voices.

Other scientists and doctors have also joined the resistance, including Dr. Michael Yeadon, former Vice President and Chief Scientist for Allergy and Respiratory at Pfizer, who has called for an end to the mass vaccination campaign and the return to normal life. He has argued that the COVID-19 vaccines are unnecessary for the vast majority of the population, as the virus poses little risk to most people.

However, these voices of dissent have faced condemnation and censorship from mainstream medical institutions and the media. Some hospitals have even fired doctors and nurses who refuse to comply with vaccine mandates, sparking outrage and protests.

Despite this, the resistance against medical tyranny continues to grow, with citizens taking to the streets to demand their rights and freedoms. Protests against vaccine mandates and vaccine passports have taken place in countries around the world, with people from all walks of life coming together to fight for their individual rights and liberties.

The resistance against medical tyranny represents a critical voice in the ongoing debate over public health and individual rights. While the medical community and government officials may argue that certain measures are necessary for public health and safety, it is important to ensure that these measures do not encroach on individual rights and freedoms. The voices of doctors, scientists, and citizens who speak out against medical tyranny must be heard and their concerns addressed, in order to maintain a healthy and just society.

One of the most prominent voices in this movement is Dr. Robert Malone, the inventor of mRNA vaccine technology, who has been vocal in his criticism of the COVID-19 vaccination campaign. Dr. Malone has expressed concerns about the lack of transparency and data sharing in the vaccine rollout, as well as the potential long-term side effects of the vaccines. He has called for a more nuanced approach to vaccination that takes into account individual risk factors and medical history.

Another notable figure in the resistance is Dr. Peter McCullough, a cardiologist and internist who has been critical of the suppression of alternative treatments for COVID-19, such as hydroxychloroquine and ivermectin. Dr. McCullough has also raised concerns about the censorship of medical information and the silencing of dissenting voices.

The resistance against medical tyranny is not limited to the medical community, however. Citizens around the world are also taking a stand against vaccine mandates and vaccine passports, which they see as an infringement on their individual rights and liberties. Protests against these measures have taken place in countries such as the United States, France, and Australia, with people from all walks of life coming together to demand their voices be heard.

Despite the growing resistance, mainstream medical institutions and the media continue to promote vaccine mandates and dismiss dissenting voices. Some hospitals and healthcare systems have even fired doctors and nurses who refuse to comply with vaccine mandates, causing outrage and protest.

It is not just about vaccines, however. It also includes concerns about the erosion of civil liberties and constitutional rights, the use of technology and surveillance to control and monitor the population, and the politicalization of science. These issues are interconnected and represent a broader concern about the balance between public health and individual rights and freedoms.

It is important for society to listen to and address the concerns of doctors, scientists, and citizens who speak out against medical tyranny, in order to ensure that measures taken to protect public health do not infringe on individual rights and liberties. Only through open dialogue and a willingness to consider multiple perspectives can we find a way forward that balances public health with individual freedom.

Chapter 12

The Implications of Lockdowns on Mental Health and Societal Well-Being

The COVID-19 pandemic has been a time of unprecedented uncertainty and disruption for many people around the world. In response to the rapid spread of the virus, governments and medical authorities implemented extreme measures to control the spread of the virus, including lockdowns. While lockdowns have been justified on the grounds of protecting public health, they have also had significant implications for mental health and societal well-being.

One of the most significant impacts of lockdowns has been on mental health. Social isolation, uncertainty, and economic stress have contributed to increased levels of anxiety, depression, and other mental health disorders. The lack of access to mental health services during lockdowns has also contributed to a potential increase in untreated mental health conditions. Moreover, some people have been unable to access healthcare due to restrictions and postponements of non-urgent medical procedures.

The impact of lockdowns on children and adolescents has also been significant. School closures and social isolation have disrupted normal childhood development, leading to potential long-term consequences. The lack of social interaction and support networks has also contributed to increased levels of anxiety and depression among young people. Additionally, the closure of schools has created challenges for working parents, and some families have had to deal with job losses and financial difficulties. Lockdowns have also had significant implications for societal well-being. The closure of businesses and other public spaces has resulted in economic hardship for many people, particularly those in low-income and marginalized communities.

The loss of social interaction and community engagement has also contributed to a sense of social disconnection and alienation. Furthermore, the impact of lockdowns has not been evenly distributed, with marginalized communities being disproportionately affected. The impact of lockdowns on mental health and societal well-being has also had implications for democracy and individual freedoms. The continuation of lockdowns raises questions about the balance between protecting public health and respecting individual freedoms.

The imposition of lockdowns without democratic oversight and public consultation raises concerns about the abuse of power and the erosion of democratic values. Overall, the implications of lockdowns on mental health and societal well-being have been significant. While lockdowns may have been necessary in the early stages of the pandemic, their continuation has raised questions about their effectiveness and proportionality. In the coming chapters, we will examine the ways in which lockdowns have impacted mental health and societal well-being, and the implications of these impacts for democracy and individual freedoms.

Chapter 13

The Impact of Lockdowns on Economic Stability and Financial Security

The COVID-19 pandemic has had a significant impact on the global economy. The rapid spread of the virus and the implementation of lockdowns have resulted in widespread business closures, job losses, and economic hardship. The impact of lockdowns on economic stability and financial security has been particularly significant, with some experts warning of a potential economic depression. Lockdowns have had a significant impact on businesses, particularly small businesses. The closure of non-essential businesses during lockdowns has resulted in reduced revenue and increased debt.

Many small businesses have been forced to close permanently, leading to job losses and economic hardship. The impact of lockdowns on small businesses has also had implications for economic inequality, as marginalized communities are more likely to be employed in small businesses. Job losses have been a significant consequence of lockdowns. The closure of non-essential businesses and restrictions on movement have resulted in reduced demand for labor. Many businesses have been forced to lay off workers or reduce their hours, leading to economic hardship for many families.

The impact of job losses has also been unevenly distributed, with marginalized communities being disproportionately affected. The economic impact of lockdowns has also had implications for financial security. The closure of businesses and job losses have resulted in increased debt and reduced savings for many people. The lack of financial security has contributed to increased stress and anxiety, particularly among those who are already marginalized or vulnerable. Furthermore, the economic impact of lockdowns has not been evenly distributed.

Wealthier individuals and corporations have been able to weather the economic storm, while marginalized communities and small businesses have borne the brunt of the economic impact. This has contributed to economic inequality and social unrest. Overall, the impact of lockdowns on economic stability and financial security has been significant.

While lockdowns may have been necessary in the early stages of the pandemic, their continuation has raised questions about their effectiveness and proportionality. In the coming chapters, we will examine the ways in which lockdowns have impacted economic stability and financial security, and the implications of these impacts for democracy and individual freedoms.

Chapter 14

The Impact of Lockdowns on Education and Learning

The COVID-19 pandemic has had a significant impact on education and learning. School closures and the implementation of remote learning have disrupted education for millions of students around the world. The impact of lockdowns on education has been particularly significant for marginalized communities, who are more likely to lack access to digital resources and support. The closure of schools during lockdowns has had a significant impact on students. Remote learning has been challenging for many students, particularly those who lack access to digital resources and support.

The lack of face-to-face interaction with teachers and peers has also had an impact on student motivation and engagement. Furthermore, the closure of schools has disrupted normal childhood development, leading to potential long-term consequences. The impact of school closures has also been unevenly distributed. Students from marginalized communities, such as low-income students and students of color, are more likely to lack access to digital resources and support, leading to greater educational disparities.

The closure of schools has also created challenges for working parents, who may struggle to balance work and childcare responsibilities. The impact of lockdowns on education has also had implications for societal well-being. The disruption of education and the potential long-term consequences of school closures can have a significant impact on future economic stability and social cohesion. Furthermore, the impact of school closures on marginalized communities can contribute to increased social inequality and exclusion. Moreover, the closure of schools has had a significant impact on the mental health of students.

Social isolation, lack of routine, and the loss of in-person support have contributed to increased levels of anxiety and depression among students. Furthermore, the lack of access to mental health services during lockdowns has contributed to a potential increase in untreated mental health conditions. Overall, the impact of lockdowns on education and learning has been significant. While remote learning may have been necessary in the early stages of the pandemic, its continuation has raised questions about its effectiveness and accessibility. In the coming chapters, we will examine the ways in which lockdowns have impacted education and learning, and the implications of these impacts for democracy and individual freedoms.

I mentioned that the closure of schools during lockdowns has had a significant impact on the mental health of students. Social isolation, lack of routine, and the loss of in-person support have contributed to increased levels of anxiety and depression among students. This has been particularly difficult for students who already struggle with mental health issues, as the lack of access to mental health services during lockdowns has contributed to a potential increase in untreated mental health conditions.

The impact of lockdowns on mental health has been particularly significant for children and adolescents. The lack of social interaction and support networks has also contributed to increased levels of anxiety and depression among young people. The disruption of education and normal childhood development can also have long-term consequences for mental health.

It is important to address the mental health implications of lockdowns and school closures. Schools and communities need to prioritize mental health support and resources for students and families during and after lockdowns. The development of online mental health resources and services can help bridge the gap in access to mental health care during lockdowns.

The promotion of healthy coping mechanisms and social connections can help mitigate the impact of social isolation on mental health. Overall, the mental health implications of lockdowns on students and young people have been significant. It is important for schools and communities to address these issues to support the well-being of students during and after lockdowns.

Chapter 15

The Role of Media in Shaping Perceptions of Lockdowns

The media has played a significant role in shaping public perceptions of lockdowns during the COVID-19 pandemic. The constant stream of news coverage and opinions has contributed to a polarized public debate on the effectiveness and proportionality of lockdowns. The role of media in shaping perceptions of lockdowns raises questions about the responsibility of media outlets and the impact of media coverage on democracy and individual freedoms.

Media coverage of lockdowns has often been sensationalized, with attention-grabbing headlines and alarmist reporting. The focus on negative aspects of lockdowns, such as economic hardship and social isolation, has contributed to a negative perception of lockdowns among the public. Furthermore, media coverage has often been politicized, with different media outlets presenting opposing views on the effectiveness and proportionality of lockdowns. The role of media in shaping public perceptions of lockdowns raises questions about the responsibility of media outlets. While media outlets have a responsibility to report on the impact of lockdowns, they also have a responsibility to provide accurate and balanced reporting.

Sensationalized reporting and biased coverage can contribute to a polarized public debate and undermine the effectiveness of democratic decision-making. The impact of media coverage on democracy and individual freedoms is also a concern. The politicization of lockdowns in the media can contribute to the erosion of trust in democratic institutions and the suppression of dissenting views. Furthermore, the constant stream of negative reporting on lockdowns can contribute to increased levels of fear and anxiety among the public, leading to a potential erosion of individual freedoms.

The role of media in shaping perceptions of lockdowns is significant. Media outlets have a responsibility to provide accurate and balanced reporting on the impact of lockdowns. The politicization of lockdowns in the media raises concerns about the impact of media coverage on democracy and individual freedoms. In the coming chapters, we will examine the ways in which media coverage has shaped perceptions of lockdowns, and the implications of these perceptions for democracy and individual freedoms.

Chapter 16

The Ethical Implications of Lockdowns

The COVID-19 pandemic has raised significant ethical questions about the use of lockdowns to contain the spread of the virus. While lockdowns may be necessary to prevent the spread of the virus and protect public health, they also raise concerns about the impact on individual freedoms and human rights. The ethical implications of lockdowns are complex and multifaceted and require careful consideration. One ethical concern related to lockdowns is the impact on individual freedoms.

Lockdowns restrict individuals' ability to move freely and engage in social activities, which raises questions about the balance between public health and individual autonomy. The use of coercive measures, such as fines and imprisonment, to enforce lockdowns also raises concerns about the use of state power to restrict individual freedoms. Another ethical concern related to lockdowns is the impact on vulnerable populations.

Lockdowns can exacerbate existing inequalities, such as access to healthcare and resources, and may have long-term consequences for marginalized communities. The ethical implications of lockdowns also include considerations of distributive justice. The burden of lockdowns is not evenly distributed, with marginalized communities and low-income individuals bearing a disproportionate share of the economic and social impacts. The allocation of resources during lockdowns, such as access to healthcare and financial support, must be done in a way that is equitable and just.

The ethical implications of lockdowns extend beyond the individual and societal level to a global level. The impact of lockdowns on low-income countries and vulnerable populations around the world must be considered in the global response to the pandemic. Overall, the ethical implications of lockdowns are complex and multifaceted.

While lockdowns may be necessary to prevent the spread of the virus and protect public health, they also raise concerns about individual freedoms, vulnerable populations, distributive justice, and global solidarity. In the coming chapters, we will examine the ethical implications of lockdowns in more detail and consider potential frameworks for ethical decision-making related to lockdowns.

The importance of transparency and accountability in decision-making related to lockdowns is essential to ensure that public health measures are balanced with individual freedoms and human rights. Overall, the ethical implications of lockdowns are complex and multifaceted. While lockdowns may be necessary to prevent the spread of the virus and protect public health, they also raise concerns about individual freedoms, vulnerable populations, distributive justice, global solidarity, and democratic decision-making. In the coming chapters, we will examine the ethical implications of lockdowns in more detail and consider potential frameworks for ethical decision-making related to lockdowns.

Chapter 17

The Impact of Lockdowns on the Economy

The COVID-19 pandemic and subsequent lockdowns have had a significant impact on the global economy. The closures of businesses and restrictions on travel and trade have resulted in job losses, decreased economic activity, and increased government spending. The impact of lockdowns on the economy is complex and multifaceted and requires a careful examination of both short-term and long-term effects.

The immediate impact of lockdowns on the economy has been significant. The closures of non-essential businesses and restrictions on travel and gatherings have led to job losses and decreased economic activity. Small businesses and industries that rely on in-person interactions have been particularly affected by lockdowns. The decrease in economic activity has also led to a decrease in tax revenues, which has made it difficult for governments to provide necessary services. The impact of lockdowns on the economy has not been evenly distributed. Low-income individuals and marginalized communities have been disproportionately affected by job losses and decreased economic activity.

The unequal distribution of economic impacts during lockdowns can exacerbate existing inequalities and lead to long-term economic and social consequences. The long-term impact of lockdowns on the economy is also significant. The closure of businesses and decrease in economic activity can have long-term consequences for economic growth and development. The increased government spending on pandemic-related programs and support can also lead to long-term economic consequences, such as increased government debt and inflation.

However, the impact of lockdowns on the economy is not limited to negative consequences. Lockdowns can also provide an opportunity for innovation and investment in new industries and technologies. The shift to remote work and online services has led to an increase in demand for digital infrastructure and technology, which can contribute to economic growth in the long-term. Overall, the impact of lockdowns on the economy is complex and multifaceted. While the immediate impact of lockdowns on the economy has been significant, the long-term consequences are still unclear. The unequal distribution of economic impacts during lockdowns raises concerns about the exacerbation of existing inequalities.

The potential for innovation and investment in new industries and technologies during lockdowns provides an opportunity for economic growth and development in the long-term. In the coming chapters, we will examine the impact of lockdowns on different sectors of the economy and consider potential strategies for economic recovery.

Chapter 18

The Impact of Lockdowns on Education

The COVID-19 pandemic and subsequent lockdowns have had a significant impact on education around the world. School closures and the shift to online learning have disrupted the education of millions of students and raised concerns about the long-term consequences of the pandemic on education. The impact of lockdowns on education is complex and multifaceted and requires a careful examination of both short-term and long-term effects. The immediate impact of lockdowns on education has been significant.

School closures and the shift to online learning have disrupted the education of millions of students, particularly those from low-income and marginalized communities. The unequal access to technology and the internet has made it difficult for some students to continue their education online. The disruption to education has also had a significant impact on mental health and well-being, particularly for students who rely on school for social support and resources.

The impact of lockdowns on education has not been limited to students. Teachers and education staff have also been affected by lockdowns, with many experiencing job losses and decreased job security. The closure of schools has also had a significant impact on parents, particularly those who have had to balance work and child care responsibilities. The long-term impact of lockdowns on education is also significant.

The disruption to education can have long-term consequences for academic achievement, employment opportunities, and social mobility.

The unequal distribution of educational impacts during lockdowns can exacerbate existing inequalities and lead to long-term consequences for social and economic development. However, the impact of lockdowns on education also provides an opportunity for innovation and investment in new educational technologies and models.

The shift to online learning has highlighted the importance of digital infrastructure and technology in education and has provided an opportunity for educators to experiment with new models of teaching and learning. Overall, the impact of lockdowns on education is complex and multifaceted. While the immediate impact of lockdowns on education has been significant, the long-term consequences are still unclear. The unequal distribution of educational impacts during lockdowns raises concerns about the exacerbation of existing inequalities.

The potential for innovation and investment in new educational technologies and models during lockdowns provides an opportunity for positive change in the long-term. In the coming chapters, we will examine the impact of lockdowns on different levels of education and consider potential strategies for educational recovery.

Chapter 19

The Impact of Lockdowns on Domestic Violence

The COVID-19 pandemic and subsequent lockdowns have had a significant impact on domestic violence around the world. The isolation, financial stress, and increased time spent at home during lockdowns have led to an increase in domestic violence incidents. The impact of lockdowns on domestic violence is complex and multifaceted and requires a careful examination of both short-term and long-term effects. The immediate impact of lockdowns on domestic violence has been significant.

The isolation and increased time spent at home during lockdowns have created a situation where victims of domestic violence are trapped with their abusers. The financial stress caused by the pandemic has also exacerbated domestic violence, as financial pressures can lead to increased tension and conflict within households. The impact of lockdowns on domestic violence has not been limited to the immediate effects.

The long-term consequences of the pandemic and lockdowns on domestic violence are still unclear, but there are concerns that the increased incidence of domestic violence during lockdowns could lead to long-term trauma and consequences for victims. Furthermore, the impact of lockdowns on domestic violence also raises questions about the role of government and society in addressing domestic violence.

The closure of domestic violence shelters and the increased pressure on domestic violence hotlines during lockdowns has made it difficult for victims to access necessary support. The unequal distribution of domestic violence impacts during lockdowns can exacerbate existing domestic violence inequalities and lead to long-term consequences for social and economic development. However, the impact of lockdowns on domestic violence also provides an opportunity for innovation and investment in domestic violence prevention and support.

The increased awareness of the importance of domestic violence prevention during the pandemic has provided an opportunity for governments and organizations to prioritize domestic violence prevention and support. The shift to telehealth and online support for domestic violence victims during lockdowns has also highlighted the importance of digital infrastructure and technology in domestic violence prevention and support. Overall, the impact of lockdowns on domestic violence is complex and multifaceted.

While the immediate impact of lockdowns on domestic violence has been significant, the long-term consequences are still unclear. The unequal distribution of domestic violence impacts during lockdowns raises concerns about the exacerbation of existing domestic violence inequalities. The potential for innovation and investment in domestic violence prevention and support during lockdowns provides an opportunity for positive change in the long-term. In the coming chapters, we will examine the impact of lockdowns on different populations and consider potential strategies for domestic violence prevention and support.

Chapter 20

Strategies for Recovery and Resilience

The COVID-19 pandemic and subsequent lockdowns have had a significant impact on all aspects of society, from the economy to education to mental health. The impact of lockdowns is complex and multifaceted and requires a comprehensive and coordinated response to address the short-term and long-term consequences.

To promote recovery and resilience in the aftermath of lockdowns, a multi-faceted approach is needed. This approach should address the various impacts of lockdowns, including those on the economy, education, mental health, domestic violence, and domestic labor. The following are potential strategies for recovery and resilience:

Investment in Economic Recovery: Governments and organizations can invest in programs to support economic recovery, including job training and support for small businesses.

Investment in Education: Governments and organizations can invest in programs to support education recovery, including support for online learning and mental health resources for students.

Investment in Mental Health: Governments and organizations can invest in mental health services and support, including telehealth and online mental health resources.

Investment in Domestic Violence Prevention and Support: Governments and organizations can invest in domestic violence prevention and support, including funding for domestic violence shelters and hotlines.

Investment in Domestic Labor Support and Empowerment: Governments and organizations can invest in programs to support domestic labor responsibilities, including support for childcare and household chores.

Prioritizing Equity: Recovery and resilience efforts should prioritize equity and address existing inequalities, including those related to race, gender, and socio-economic status.

Community Engagement: Recovery and resilience efforts should engage with local communities to identify and address their specific needs and concerns.

International Cooperation: Recovery and resilience efforts should involve international cooperation and collaboration to address the global impact of the pandemic and lockdowns.

A comprehensive and coordinated approach is needed to promote recovery and resilience in the aftermath of lockdowns. The strategies outlined above can serve as a starting point for governments and organizations to address the various impacts of lockdowns and promote positive change in the long-term.

In addition to the strategies mentioned in this previous chapter, there are several other potential strategies for recovery and resilience in the aftermath of lockdowns.

Investment in Infrastructure: Governments and organizations can invest in infrastructure projects to support economic recovery, such as transportation and broadband infrastructure.

Investment in Healthcare: Governments and organizations can invest in healthcare systems and resources to better prepare for future pandemics and to address the long-term health consequences of the pandemic.

Promoting Sustainable Development: Recovery and resilience efforts should prioritize sustainable development and address environmental concerns, such as climate change and the depletion of natural resources.

Strengthening Social Safety Nets: Governments and organizations can strengthen social safety nets, such as unemployment insurance and food assistance programs, to support those most affected by the pandemic and lockdowns.

Promoting Innovation: Recovery and resilience efforts should promote innovation and entrepreneurship to foster new economic opportunities and address existing challenges.

Supporting International Development: Recovery and resilience efforts should include support for international development and assistance to countries most affected by the pandemic and lockdowns.

Encouraging Community Resilience: Recovery and resilience efforts should encourage community resilience by promoting community engagement, social cohesion, and community-based solutions.

Recovery and resilience efforts in the aftermath of lockdowns should be comprehensive and include a range of strategies to address the various impacts of the pandemic and lockdowns. These strategies should prioritize equity, sustainability, and community resilience, and should involve collaboration and cooperation at the local, national, and international levels. By adopting a multi-faceted approach, governments and organizations can promote recovery and resilience in the aftermath of lockdowns and create a more just, sustainable, and resilient world.

Chapter 21

Possible Negative Effects of Current Human Trials for an RSV-Flu-COVID Vaccine

The development of a combined vaccine for respiratory syncytial virus (RSV), influenza (flu), and COVID-19 has been underway since the start of the pandemic. While a combined vaccine may seem like an ideal solution to protect against multiple respiratory viruses, there are potential negative effects that must be carefully considered. One concern is the potential for increased vaccine side effects.

Vaccines for RSV and flu are known to have side effects, including fever, headache, and muscle pain. These side effects can be more severe in some individuals, particularly those with a weakened immune system or other underlying health conditions. Combining a RSV-flu-COVID vaccine may increase the likelihood and severity of these side effects, which could deter individuals from getting vaccinated. Another concern is the potential for decreased vaccine efficacy.

Each of the three viruses in the combined vaccine is distinct, and each requires a unique immune response for protection. Combining multiple vaccines into one may reduce the efficacy of each individual vaccine, as the immune response may be diluted or compromised. This could result in decreased protection against each individual virus, and could also have implications for future outbreaks or mutations of these viruses. The timing of the RSV-flu-COVID vaccine trials is also a concern. With the COVID-19 pandemic still ongoing, the focus on developing a vaccine for COVID-19 has taken priority over other vaccines.

This has resulted in expedited clinical trials for the RSV-flu-COVID vaccine, which may not allow for thorough testing and evaluation of potential negative effects. Additionally, the rush to develop a combined vaccine may also result in limited access and distribution to populations in need. Developing and producing a combined vaccine requires significant resources and technology, which may not be available in all countries or to all populations.

This could further exacerbate existing inequities in access to healthcare and vaccines. While the development of a RSV-flu-COVID vaccine is promising, it is important to carefully consider the potential negative effects and implications. Further research and evaluation of the vaccine is needed to ensure its safety and efficacy, and to address concerns about vaccine side effects, decreased efficacy, and limited access. It is also important to prioritize equitable distribution and access to the vaccine, particularly for vulnerable populations.

Chapter 22

The Possible Negative Effects of Adding a COVID Vaccine or RSV-Flu-COVID Vaccine to the Mandatory Vaccine Schedule for School Children

As vaccines for COVID-19 and a RSV-flu-COVID triple vaccine continue to be developed and distributed, there are concerns about the possibility of adding these vaccines to the mandatory vaccine schedule for school children. While mandatory vaccinations have been shown to be effective in preventing the spread of infectious diseases, there are potential negative effects that must be considered before adding a COVID or triple vaccine to the schedule.

One concern is the potential for vaccine hesitancy and opposition. The COVID-19 pandemic has already highlighted the significant amount of vaccine hesitancy and opposition in some populations. Adding a COVID or triple vaccine to the mandatory vaccine schedule for school children may further exacerbate this issue, particularly among parents who are already hesitant about vaccines. This could result in decreased vaccine uptake and potential outbreaks of preventable diseases.

Another concern is the potential for vaccine side effects. While vaccines are generally safe and effective, they can have side effects, particularly in certain individuals. Adding a COVID or triple vaccine to the mandatory vaccine schedule may increase the likelihood of vaccine side effects, particularly if the vaccines are given in close proximity to each other.

The cost of adding a COVID or triple vaccine to the mandatory vaccine schedule is also a concern. Vaccines can be expensive and adding a COVID or triple vaccine to the mandatory schedule could result in increased costs for schools and families. This could further exacerbate existing inequities in access to healthcare and vaccines, particularly for low-income families. Furthermore, there are concerns about the potential long-term effects of these vaccines, particularly in children.

While the short-term safety and efficacy of COVID and triple vaccines have been studied, the long-term effects are still unknown. Adding these vaccines to the mandatory schedule could result in unintended consequences, particularly for children who may be more vulnerable to the effects of the vaccine.

Overall, while adding a COVID or triple vaccine to the mandatory vaccine schedule for school children may seem like a logical solution to prevent the spread of infectious diseases, there are potential negative effects that must be carefully considered. These include vaccine hesitancy and opposition, vaccine side effects, increased costs, and potential long-term effects. It is important to carefully evaluate the safety and efficacy of these vaccines before adding them to the mandatory vaccine schedule, and to prioritize equitable access and distribution to ensure that all children have access to life-saving vaccines.

The COVID-19 pandemic and subsequent lockdowns have had a profound impact on all aspects of society, from the economy to education to mental health. The impact of lockdowns is complex and multifaceted and requires a comprehensive and coordinated response to address the short-term and long-term consequences. In this book, we have examined the various impacts of lockdowns, including those on the economy, education, mental health, domestic violence, and domestic labor.

We have also discussed potential strategies for recovery and resilience in the aftermath of lockdowns, including investment in economic recovery, education, mental health, domestic violence prevention and support, domestic labor support and empowerment, equity, community engagement, and international cooperation.

The COVID-19 pandemic and lockdowns have highlighted the interconnectedness and vulnerability of our global society. It has also highlighted the importance of collaboration and cooperation at the local, national, and international levels to address global challenges.

As we move forward in the aftermath of lockdowns, it is important to prioritize sustainability, equity, and community resilience in our recovery and resilience efforts. By adopting a multi-faceted and collaborative approach, we can create a more just, sustainable, and resilient world. It is our hope that this book will contribute to ongoing discussions and efforts to address the impact of lockdowns and promote recovery and resilience in the aftermath of the COVID-19 pandemic.

Chapter 23

The Future of Medical Tyranny and What We Can Do About It

The issue of medical tyranny is one that requires continued vigilance, as the potential for abuse is ever present. The COVID-19 pandemic has brought this issue to the forefront of public consciousness, but it is important to recognize that it is a much broader and more pervasive problem than just one virus. As we move forward, there are several key areas that we must focus on in order to prevent the spread of medical tyranny and protect our civil liberties.

First and foremost, it is essential that we remain vigilant in monitoring the actions of government and private entities in the healthcare sector. This includes paying attention to legislation and executive orders that could potentially infringe on our rights, as well as scrutinizing the policies and practices of healthcare providers to ensure that they are not overstepping their bounds.

Secondly, we must continue to support and amplify the voices of those who are speaking out against medical tyranny. This includes doctors, scientists, and citizens who are working tirelessly to raise awareness about the dangers of excessive government and corporate control in the healthcare sector. By providing a platform for these voices and actively advocating for their cause, we can help to create a more informed and engaged public.

Thirdly, we must remain committed to holding those who engage in medical tyranny accountable for their actions. This includes filing legal challenges against unconstitutional policies and practices, as well as using the power of public opinion to pressure lawmakers and businesses to change their behavior. By making it clear that there will be consequences for those who violate our civil liberties, we can help to deter future abuses.

Finally, we must be proactive in working to create a healthcare system that prioritizes individual autonomy and informed consent. This includes advocating for patient-centered care models, promoting education and awareness about healthcare options and alternatives, and pushing for greater transparency and accountability in the healthcare industry. By working to build a system that is truly focused on the needs and rights of patients, we can help to ensure that medical tyranny is never allowed to take root.

In conclusion, the issue of medical tyranny is one that requires continued attention and action from all of us. By remaining vigilant, supporting those who are speaking out, holding violators accountable, and working to create a better healthcare system, we can help to safeguard our civil liberties and prevent the spread of medical tyranny both now and in the future.

Chapter 24

The Need for a Paradigm Shift in Public Health Policies and Approaches

The COVID-19 pandemic has highlighted the need for a paradigm shift in public health policies and approaches. The traditional model of responding to public health crises has focused primarily on controlling the spread of infectious diseases through measures such as quarantine, contact tracing, and vaccination campaigns. While these measures are important, they do not address the underlying causes of many public health problems, including chronic diseases, environmental factors, and social determinants of health.

To effectively address these issues, a new paradigm is needed that shifts the focus from treating illness to promoting wellness and preventing disease. This new approach should be holistic, addressing not only physical health but also mental, emotional, and social well-being.

One of the key components of this new paradigm is a focus on prevention rather than treatment. This means promoting healthy behaviors, such as regular physical activity, healthy eating, and stress reduction, as well as addressing environmental factors that contribute to poor health outcomes, such as pollution and access to healthy food.

Another important component of the new paradigm is a focus on social determinants of health, such as poverty, education, and access to healthcare. These factors have a significant impact on health outcomes and addressing them is essential to promoting health equity and reducing health disparities.

The medical community has an important role to play in advocating for this new paradigm and working with policymakers to implement policies and programs that support it. This includes investing in research to better understand the underlying causes of health problems and developing effective prevention and treatment strategies.

Citizens also have a role to play in promoting this new paradigm by advocating for policies that support health and wellness and by making healthy choices in their own lives.

The COVID-19 pandemic has highlighted the need for a paradigm shift in public health policies and approaches. To effectively address the underlying causes of many public health problems, a new holistic approach that focuses on prevention, social determinants of health, and wellness is needed. The medical community, policymakers, and citizens all have a role to play in promoting this new paradigm and working together to build a healthier, more equitable society.

Chapter 25

Moving Forward: The Importance of Freedom, Transparency, and Accountability in Medical Practices

Medical practices are an essential aspect of society, and they play a vital role in ensuring the health and well-being of individuals. However, the events of the COVID-19 pandemic have highlighted the need for more transparency and accountability in medical practices. The pandemic has revealed that there is a lack of trust between the public and the medical community, and this has led to concerns about the safety and efficacy of medical treatments and practices.

Moving forward, it is essential that we focus on promoting freedom, transparency, and accountability in medical practices. These principles are crucial for ensuring that individuals have the right to make informed decisions about their health and well-being. It is also essential for building trust between the public and the medical community.

Freedom is an essential aspect of medical practices. Individuals should have the freedom to choose their medical treatments and make informed decisions about their health. This requires that medical practitioners provide accurate and comprehensive information about medical treatments and procedures, as well as their potential risks and benefits. Individuals should also have the freedom to access alternative treatments and therapies that are safe and effective.

Transparency is also critical for building trust between the public and the medical community. Medical practitioners and institutions should be transparent about their practices, policies, and procedures. This includes providing accurate and comprehensive information about medical treatments and procedures, as well as their potential risks and benefits. It also includes being transparent about any conflicts of interest that may exist, such as financial ties to pharmaceutical companies.

Accountability is also essential for ensuring that medical practices are safe and effective. Medical practitioners and institutions should be held accountable for any errors or mistakes that occur. This requires that there are clear standards of care and regulations in place to ensure that medical practices are safe and effective. It also requires that there are mechanisms in place to hold medical practitioners and institutions accountable when these standards are not met.

Moving forward, it is essential that we focus on promoting freedom, transparency, and accountability in medical practices. These principles are essential for ensuring that individuals have the right to make informed decisions about their health and well-being. They are also critical for building trust between the public and the medical community. By promoting these principles, we can work towards a future where medical practices are safe, effective, and trusted by the public.

Sources

CENTERS FOR DISEASE Control and Prevention. (2021). COVID-19: Cases, Data, and Surveillance. Retrieved from https://www.cdc.gov/coronavirus/2019-ncov/cases-updates/index.html

World Health Organization. (2021). Coronavirus disease (COVID-19) pandemic. Retrieved from https://www.who.int/emergencies/disease/novel-coronavirus-2019

Marmot, M., & Allen, J. (2020). COVID-19: exposing and amplifying inequalities. Journal of Epidemiology and Community Health, 74(9), 681-682.

Van Lancker, W., & Parolin, Z. (2020). COVID-19, school closures, and child poverty: a social crisis in the making. The Lancet Public Health, 5(5), e243-e244.

Viner, R. M., Russell, S. J., Croker, H., Packer, J., Ward, J., Stansfield, C., & Mytton, O. (2020). School closure and management practices during coronavirus outbreaks including COVID-19: a rapid systematic review. The Lancet Child & Adolescent Health, 4(5), 397-404.

Nacoti, M., Ciocca, A., Giupponi, A., Brambillasca, P., Lussana, F., Pisano, M., & Goisis, G. (2020). At the epicenter of the Covid-19 pandemic and humanitarian crises in Italy: changing perspectives on preparation and mitigation. NEJM Catalyst, 1(2).

UNICEF. (2020). COVID-19: Are children able to continue learning during school closures? A global analysis of the potential reach of remote learning policies. Retrieved from https://data.unicef.org/resources/remote-learning-reachability-factsheet/

De Silva, M. J., Rathod, S. D., Hanlon, C., Breuer, E., Chisholm, D., Fekadu, A., & Lund, C. (2020). Evaluation of district mental healthcare plans: the PRIME consortium methodology. The British Journal of Psychiatry, 216(1), 29-37.

Aldridge, R. W., Lewer, D., Katikireddi, S. V., Mathur, R., Pathak, N., Burns, R., & Hayward, A. (2020). Black, Asian and Minority Ethnic groups in England are at increased risk of death from COVID-19: indirect standardisation of NHS mortality data. Wellcome Open Research, 5(88).

Bhatia, R., Wallace, S., & Wurzel, G. (2020). Pediatric otolaryngology and COVID-19: the impact on providers and patients. International Journal of Pediatric Otorhinolaryngology, 138, 110338.

Recommended Reading

The Lancet COVID-19 Commission Statement on the occasion of the 75th session of the UN General Assembly. The Lancet, 396(10257), 1102-1124.

World Health Organization. (2020). Mental health and psychosocial considerations during the COVID-19 outbreak. Retrieved from https://www.who.int/docs/default-source/coronaviruse/mental-health-considerations.pdf

United Nations. (2020). Policy Brief: Education during COVID-19 and beyond. Retrieved from https://www.un.org/sites/un2.un.org/files/sg_policy_brief_covid-19_and_education

UNESCO. (2020). COVID-19 impact on education. Retrieved from https://en.unesco.org/covid19/educationresponse

World Health Organization. (2020). Transmission of SARS-CoV-2: implications for infection prevention precautions. Retrieved from https://www.who.int/news-room/commentaries/detail/transmission-of-sars-cov-2-implications-for-infection-prevention-precautions

Centers for Disease Control and Prevention. (2020). Interim guidance for administrators of US K-12 schools and childcare programs to plan, prepare, and respond to coronavirus disease 2019 (COVID-19). Retrieved from https://www.cdc.gov/coronavirus/2019-ncov/community/schools-childcare/guidance-for-schools.html

The New York Times. (2020). Coronavirus in the U.S.: Latest Map and Case Count. Retrieved from https://www.nytimes.com/interactive/2020/us/coronavirus-us-cases.html

National Institute of Mental Health. (2020). Mental Health Information: Coronavirus. Retrieved from https://www.nimh.nih.gov/health/topics/coronavirus/index.shtml

American Academy of Pediatrics. (2020). COVID-19 Interim Guidance: Return to Sports. Retrieved from https://services.aap.org/en/pages/2019-novel-coronavirus-covid-19-infections/clinical-guidance/covid-19-interim-guidance-return-to-sports/

Johns Hopkins Medicine. (2020). COVID-19: Coronavirus Resources. Retrieved from https://www.hopkinsmedicine.org/coronavirus/

Additional Sources

Dr. Robert Malone. (2021). LinkedIn Profile. Retrieved from https://www.linkedin.com/in/rwmalonemd/

Brownstone Institute. (2021). The Risks of Rushed Vaccine Approval. Retrieved from https://brownstone.org/articles/the-risks-of-rushed-vaccine-approval/

McCullough, P. A., Kelly, R. J., Ruocco, G., Lerma, E., Tumlin, J., Wheelan, K. R., & Katz, N. (2020). Pathophysiological Basis and Rationale for Early Outpatient Treatment of SARS-CoV-2 (COVID-19) Infection. The American Journal of Medicine, 133(9), 1037-1046.

Bhakdi, S., & Reiss, K. (2021). Corona, False Alarm? Facts and Figures. Chelsea Green Publishing.

Yeadon, M. (2021). Perspectives on the Pandemic | Episode 13: Interview with Dr. Michael Yeadon. Retrieved from https://www.bitchute.com/video/1pI5CPVqKjwB/

These sources include Dr. Robert Malone and other experts who have reached similar conclusions regarding the COVID-19 vaccine and related policies. Dr. Malone is a prominent vaccine researcher and inventor of mRNA vaccine technology and has been outspoken about the need for more rigorous safety testing and transparency in the development and distribution of COVID-19 vaccines. The other sources include experts in medicine, epidemiology, and public health who have also raised concerns about the safety and efficacy of COVID-19 vaccines, as well as the potential negative effects of vaccine mandates and other related policies.

Author

Mike Morton is a former infantry and SWAT medic and who retired as a Law Enforcement Officer, serving since 1994. He has achieved advanced Police Certification in Oregon, Washington, and Colorado. He holds an MA from the University of Arizona in Tucson.

He has 35 years' experience with firearms and over 40 years' experience in Martial Arts/Combatives training. As a street cop, he has an abundance of practical experience.

Mike is currently a Security and Risk Analysis consultant and private contractor for police training both in the USA and foreign countries.

He has attended and successfully completed training in military and police special weapons and tactics courses, advanced defensive tactics as well as numerous counterdrug and counter terrorist special trainings.

A prolific writer, he focuses on continual self-improvement, i.e., "failing better", as well as socio-economic and geo-political topics.

Mike is married, with two daughters. He resides in Colombia

Don't miss out!

Visit the website below and you can sign up to receive emails whenever Michael Morton publishes a new book. There's no charge and no obligation.

https://books2read.com/r/B-A-VGEX-ERQGC

BOOKS 2 READ

Connecting independent readers to independent writers.

Also by Michael Morton

Personal Autonomy Now!
Situational Awareness

Standalone
How To Raise An Alpha Child
52 Weeks to a New You! A One-Year Plan To Improve and Change
Your Life
Medical Tyranny: How Covid-19 Has Been Used to Suppress Our
Freedoms
Guía de Supervivencia Urbana
Guide de Survie en Milieu Urbain en Période de Turbulences
El Auge de la Ola Roja: La expansión de los Gobiernos Socialistas en
Sudamérica

About the Author

MIKE MORTON –

Mike is a former infantry and SWAT medic and has recently retired as a Law Enforcement Officer, serving since 1994. He has achieved advanced Police Certification in Oregon, Washington, and Colorado. He holds an MA from the University of Arizona in Tucson.

Mike has 35 years' experience with firearms and over 40 years' experience in Martial Arts/Combatives training. As a street cop, he has an abundance of practical experience.

He is currently a Security and Risk Analysis consultant and private contractor for police training both in the USA and foreign countries.

He has attended and successfully completed training in military and police special weapons and tactics courses, advanced defensive tactics as well as numerous counterdrug and counter terrorist special trainings.

Mike is the daughter of two fiercely independent, confident, Alpha females.